CW01304745

My Dog's Life
Scrapbook and Journal

Hungarian Vizsla

Capture the special moments!

Until one has loved a dog a part
of one's heart remains unawakened

A dog journal scrapbook to
document your dog's life as it happens!

*Puppies and dogs are earthly miracles with wagging tails,
little hearts full of love and the pitter-patter of paws.*

Copyright © 2015
By Debbie Miller

This dog memory book is © copyrighted by the author, Debbie Miller and is protected under the US Copyright Act of 1976 and all other applicable international, federal, state and local laws, with ALL rights reserved.

This book contains protected material. No part of this may be copied, or changed in any format, sold, or used in any way. Any unauthorized reprint or use of this material is prohibited, including photocopying, recording, or by any information storage and retrieval system without written permission from the author or publisher.

Find more unique, original dog baby books at dogjournals.com
Children baby memory books at babyfirstyearbooks.com

A Dog Journal and Scrapbook

A journal and scrapbook for your dog to keep heart filled memories and photos of special moments with your dog. There is space for lots of snapshots of your dog! This blank memory book gives dog lovers a place to chart their dog's growth.

As your dog grows into an adult you can create a book full of memories and capture the special moments.

There is a page for your dog's first birthday, first Christmas, first bath plus birth information. Keep track of your dog's vaccine records and health.

There is even a page to place your dog's paw prints!

You can take photos of your dog discovering his world as he grows into an adult.

Pictures are worth a thousand words, it helps us remember the little moments that bring us such joy in an instant.

Don't miss the special times when your dog is sleeping, bounding across the yard, their first birthday or favorite things to do! With this dog memory book you will be able to keep your favorite memories to enjoy the happy moments for years!

Start creating lasting memories today of your puppy or dog!

Yesterday I was a dog. Today I'm a dog.
Tomorrow I'll probably still be a dog.
Sigh! There's so little hope for advancement.

~Charles M. Schulz

My First Day Home

Date I joined my new family: ________________________

My First Selfie

Photo Here

My First Week Home

My Birthday: ______________________________

Place of Birth: ______________________________

Fur and Markings: ______________________________

My Name: ______________________________

I'm growing. How much did I grow!

Age	Lbs	Oz
6 Weeks		
8 Weeks		
10 Weeks		
3 Months		
4 Months		
6 Months		
8 Months		
10 Months		
1 Year		
2 Years		

Puppy Paw Print

Adult Paw Print

My Favorite Person

Photo Here

My First Bath

Photo Here

My Favorite Food

Photo Here

My Favorite Toy

Photo Here

My First Birthday

Photo Here

My First Christmas

Photo Here

Vaccination Records

Age	Date	Distemper	Parvo	Rabies	Deworm
6 weeks					
10 weeks					
14 weeks					
1 Year					
2 Years					
3 Years					
4 Years					
5 Years					
6 Years					
7 Years					
8 Years					
9 Years					
10 Years					
11 Years					
12 Years					

Heartworm Testing:

1 Year___ 2 Year___ 3 Year ___ 4 Year___ 5 Year___

6 Year___ 7 Year___ 8 Year ___ 9 Year___ 10 Year___

Medical Record Notes:

Medical Record Notes:

Medical Record Notes:

Medical Record Notes:

Medical Treatments:

Neutered	Spayed	Other

Medical Conditions:

Date	**Accidents or Injuries**

Medical Emergencies:

Medical Emergencies:

The Puppy Days

The journey of a single memory starts with a photo!
Create lasting memories today!

Our Adorable Puppy

Photo Here

Our Adorable Puppy

Photo Here

Our Adorable Puppy

Photo Here

Our Adorable Puppy

Photo Here

Our Adorable Puppy

Photo Here

Our Adorable Puppy

Photo Here

Our Adorable Puppy

Photo Here

Our Adorable Puppy

Photo Here

Our Adorable Puppy

Photo Here

Our Adorable Puppy

Photo Here

Our Adorable Puppy

Photo Here

Our Adorable Puppy

Photo Here

Our Adorable Puppy

Photo Here

Our Adorable Puppy

Photo Here

Our Adorable Puppy

Photo Here

Our Adorable Puppy

Photo Here

Our Adorable Puppy

Photo Here

Our Adorable Puppy

Photo Here

Our Adorable Puppy

Photo Here

Our Adorable Puppy

Photo Here

Our Adorable Puppy

Photo Here

Our Adorable Puppy

Photo Here

Our Adorable Puppy

Photo Here

Our Adorable Puppy

Photo Here

Our Adorable Puppy

Photo Here

Our Adorable Puppy

Photo Here

Our Adorable Puppy

Photo Here

Our Adorable Puppy

Photo Here

Our Adorable Puppy

Photo Here

Our Adorable Puppy

Photo Here

Our Adorable Puppy

Photo Here

Our Adorable Puppy

Photo Here

Our Adorable Puppy

Photo Here

Our Adorable Puppy

Photo Here

Our Adorable Puppy

Photo Here

Our Adorable Puppy

Photo Here

All Grown Up

Don't miss the special moments!
The journey of a single memory starts with a photo!

All Grown Up

Photo Here

All Grown Up

Photo Here

All Grown Up

Photo Here

All Grown Up

Photo Here

All Grown Up

Photo Here

All Grown Up

Photo Here

All Grown Up

Photo Here

All Grown Up

Photo Here

All Grown Up

Photo Here

All Grown Up

Photo Here

All Grown Up

Photo Here

All Grown Up

Photo Here

All Grown Up

Photo Here

All Grown Up

Photo Here

All Grown Up

Photo Here

All Grown Up

Photo Here

All Grown Up

Photo Here

All Grown Up

Photo Here

All Grown Up

Photo Here

All Grown Up

Photo Here

All Grown Up

Photo Here

All Grown Up

Photo Here

All Grown Up

Photo Here

All Grown Up

Photo Here

All Grown Up

Photo Here

All Grown Up

Photo Here

All Grown Up

Photo Here

All Grown Up

Photo Here

All Grown Up

Photo Here

All Grown Up

Photo Here

All Grown Up

Photo Here

All Grown Up

Photo Here

All Grown Up

Photo Here

All Grown Up

Photo Here

All Grown Up

Photo Here

All Grown Up

Photo Here

All Grown Up

Photo Here

All Grown Up

Photo Here

22912501R00059

Printed in Great Britain
by Amazon